W9-COM-776

J297 PEN

Discovering Religions

ISLAM

Sue Penney

RSVP

**RAINTREE
STECK-VAUGHN**
P U B L I S H E R S
The Steck-Vaughn Company

Austin, Texas

Published by Raintree Steck-Vaughn Publishers, an imprint of Steck-Vaughn Company

Library of Congress Cataloging-in-Publication Data

    Penney, Sue.
    Islam / Sue Penney.
       p. cm. — (Discovering religions)
    Includes index.
    ISBN 0-8172-4394-1
    1. Islam—Juvenile literature.   I. Title.   II. Series.
    BP161.2.P46 1997
    297—dc20   96-3729
                                CIP
                                AC

Religious Studies consultants: W. Owen Cole and Steven L. Ware (Drew University).

Thanks are due to E.H. Bladon for reading and advising on the manuscript.

Designed by Visual Image
Illustrated by Visual Image
Typeset by Tom Fenton Studio
Cover design by Amy Atkinson
Printed in Great Britain
Bound in the United States
1 2 3 4 5 6 7 8 9 0 WO 99 98 97 96 95

Acknowledgments

The author and publishers would like to thank the following for permission to use materials for which they hold the copyright:

Abdullah Yusuf Ali for the excerpts on pp. 7, 11, 13, 17, 19, 23, 27, 37, 39 and 47 from *Roman Transliteration of the Holy Qur'an,* published by Sh. Muhammad Ashraf, Lahore, Pakistan; Cambridge University Press for the excerpt on p. 29 from *The Islamic World: Beliefs and Civilisations, 600–1600,* Cambridge History Programme, 1993 by Peter and Ruth Mantin, and for the adapted excerpts from *The Cambridge Illustrated History of the Middle Ages,* Volume 1 on p. 33; Ruqaiyyah Waris Maqsood for the recipe for Id on p. 25 and for "Comments from a British Muslim Woman" on p. 43; The Muslim Educational Trust for "The importance of telling the truth" on p. 41 that is an abridged excerpt from *Islam for Younger People* by Ghulum Sarwar.

The publishers would like to thank the following for permission to use photos:

Cover photograph by Robert Harding Picture Library.

The Ancient Art and Architecture Collection p. 32; Kayte Brimacombe/Network p. 16; Circa Photo Library pp. 24 (below), 41; Sally and Richard Greenhill p. 7; Robert Harding Picture Library pp. 26, 33, 34 (left); The Hutchison Library p. 39; Christine Osborne Pictures p. 38; Peter Sanders pp. 8, 9, 10, 11, 12, 13, 15, 17, 18, 19, 20 (top), 23, 24 (top), 35, 36, 37, 40, 42, 43, 44, 45, 46, 47; Frank Spooner Pictures p. 31; Zefa pp. 6, 20 (below), 22, 29, 34 (right).

The publishers have made every effort to trace copyright holders. However, if any material has been incorrectly acknowledged, we would be pleased to correct this at the earliest opportunity.

CONTENTS

MAP: WHERE THE MAIN RELIGIONS BEGAN

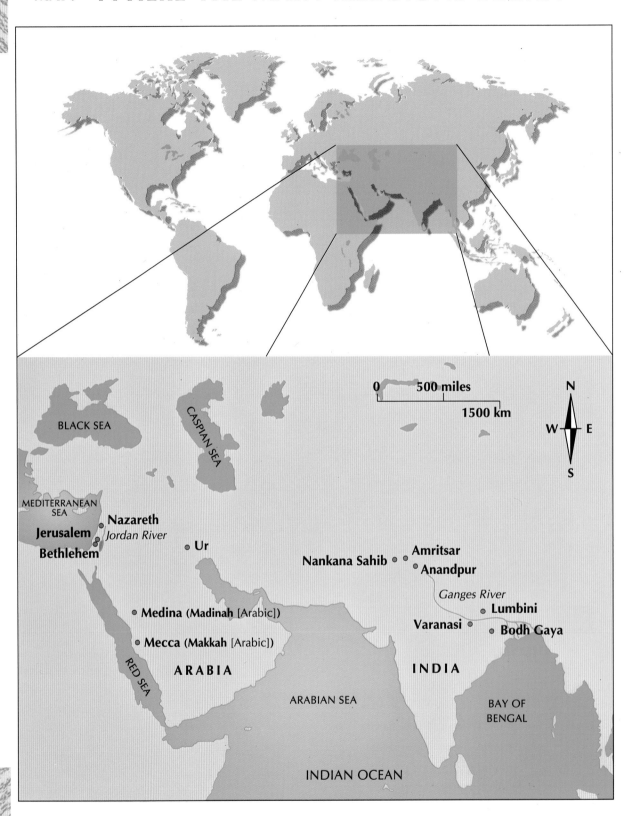

BLACK SEA

CASPIAN SEA

MEDITERRANEAN
SEA

Nazareth
Jordan River

Jerusalem

Bethlehem

Ur

Nankana Sahib

Amritsar

Anandpur

Ganges River

Medina (Madinah [Arabic])

Lumbini

Varanasi

Bodh Gaya

Mecca (Makkah [Arabic])

RED SEA

ARABIA

INDIA

ARABIAN SEA

BAY OF
BENGAL

INDIAN OCEAN

0   500 miles

1500 km

N
W   E
S

TIME CHART: WHEN THE MAIN RELIGIONS BEGAN

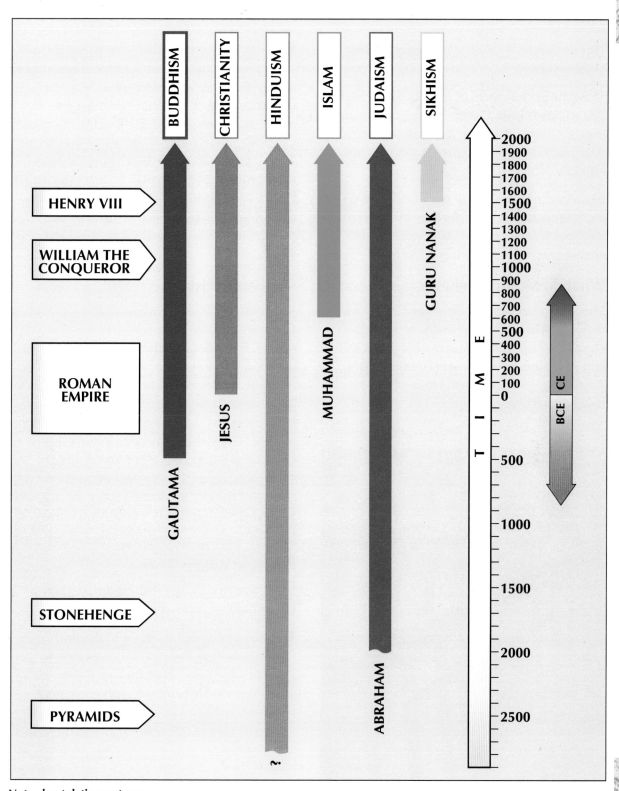

Note about dating systems

In this book dates are not called BC and AD which is the Christian dating system. The letters BCE and CE are used instead. BCE stands for Before the Common Era and CE stands for Common Era. BCE and CE can be used by people of all religions, Christians too. The year numbers are not changed.

INTRODUCING ISLAM

This section tells you something about who Muslims are.

Muslims are followers of the religion of Islam. The words "Muslim" and "Islam" both come from an Arabic word which means **submission.** A Muslim is therefore someone who has submitted to God.

Islam began in the part of the world now called the Middle East. Many Muslims still live in this area, but today there are Muslims living in almost every country in the world.

What do Muslims believe?

Muslims believe that there is one God, whom they call **Allah.** They believe that Allah is **eternal**, which means he was never born and will never die. He made everything, knows everything, and is all-powerful, so human beings must worship him.

Muslims believe that Allah sent **prophets** to teach people how to live. A prophet is someone who tells people what God wants. For Muslims, the last and most important prophet was a man called Muhammad. He lived in the country now called Saudi Arabia, and was born in 570 CE. Muslims believe that Muhammad received messages from Allah through the **Angel Gabriel** (sometimes spelled Jibril). These messages were collected together to form the Muslim holy book. This book is called the **Koran**.

Symbols for Islam

Muslims do not use **symbols** in the way that followers of some other religions do. When a symbol is needed for Islam, the one most often used is a star and crescent moon. This is found on many **mosques** and on the flags of some Muslim countries. The crescent moon is the new moon, and so is a symbol of the new lunar month. (The Muslim calendar follows the changes of the moon.) When the symbol is used on mosques, the crescent points in the direction of the city of Mecca. Mecca is a holy city for Muslims, and this is where Muhammad was born.

Points to notice

There are two things that are important to notice before you read any further.

■ Muslims do not worship Muhammad. They believe that only Allah should be worshiped, and Muhammad was not Allah. However, Muhammad is given great respect as Allah's most important prophet and, to show this, whenever they mention

The star and crescent moon is sometimes used as a symbol for Islam.

Arabic writing at the entrance to a mosque.

Muhammad's name, Muslims add the words "peace be upon him." When written, this is sometimes shortened to "pbuh."

■ The language of Islam is Arabic. To be understood by people who cannot read it, Arabic words have to be changed into other alphabets. The sounds of letters in English are not the same as the sounds of Arabic letters, so sometimes different spellings are used. For example, Muhammad can be spelled Mahomet, and Mecca can be spelled Makkah.

NEW WORDS

Allah Arabic name for God, used by all Muslims.

Angel Gabriel Messenger of Allah.

Arabic Language used in Muslim worship and spoken by some Muslims.

Eternal Lasting for ever.

Mosque Muslim place of worship.

Muslim Follower of the religion of Islam.

Prophet Someone who tells people what Allah wants.

Koran Muslim holy book.

Submission The act of yielding—obeying someone else's authority.

Symbol Something that stands for something else.

BEING A MUSLIM

It is not righteousness

That you turn your faces

Toward east or west;

But it is righteousness —

To believe in Allah,

And the Last Day,

And the Angels,

And the Book,

And the Messengers ...

To be steadfast in prayer,

And practice regular charity.

To fulfill the promises which you have made.

Surah 2 : 177

THE LIFE OF MUHAMMAD

This section tells you something about Islam's most important prophet.

Muhammad was born in a city called Mecca, in what is today called Saudi Arabia. He was born in about the year 570 CE. Muhammad had a very hard childhood. His father died just before he was born. His mother died when he was only six years old. He was brought up by his grandfather and then his uncle. When he grew up, Muhammad helped his uncle in his work as a merchant.

As a young man, Muhammad was already well known for his honesty and goodness. He worked in Mecca for a wealthy woman called Khadijah. She was a trader. When Muhammad was 25, he and Khadijah were married. They were rich and respected, their marriage was very happy—it seemed that Muhammad had everything which he could possibly want. However, he became more and more worried by the things which he saw going on in Mecca. It was a center of trade, with many wealthy people. Muhammad saw rich merchants cheating the poor, and people spending their time gambling, drinking, and fighting. **Idol** worship was common, and often included **sacrifices**. Muhammad was sure that these things were wrong. He felt that he needed to be alone to think and began going to the mountains outside Mecca to **meditate**.

One night in the year 610 CE, Muhammad was meditating in a cave on Mount Hira when he had a **vision**. In his vision, an angel came to him carrying a piece of cloth on which words were written. The angel said, "Recite!" Muhammad said that he could not read. The angel repeated the command, and Muhammad found that he was able to understand the words and read them aloud. He stood up and walked out of the cave, and heard the angel saying, "Muhammad! You are Allah's messenger!"

Muhammad was terrified by this experience. He returned home and told Khadijah about it, and she comforted him, and was the first person to believe his message came from Allah. Muhammad began preaching to people in Mecca, but he became unpopular. Most people did not want to turn away from worship of idols. Although a few people believed what Muhammad was telling them, most did not like being told they were wicked sinners. Many people were against him, so in 622 CE Muhammad accepted an invitation from the people in the nearby town of Medina. They had heard about his preaching and asked him to come and teach them.

Mecca and Mount Hira' today.

The Mosque of the Prophet in Medina.

The hijrah

Muhammad's move to Medina is called the **hijrah**. This is an Arabic word that means departure. Muslims think that this is very important, because it was the beginning of the success of Islam. The Muslim calendar begins from this date, and years are numbered AH, which means "the year of the hijrah."

While Muhammad was living in Medina, there were battles with the people of Mecca. This was because Muhammad was trying to stop people from doing things that were wrong. At last, the people of Mecca were defeated in 629 CE, and Muhammad returned in triumph. The Meccans accepted Islam as their religion, and all the idols and statues were taken out of the city. Muhammad returned to Medina, and spent the rest of his life teaching the people there. He died in 632 CE, and was buried in his house in Medina. The Mosque of the Prophet now extends over his grave.

NEW WORDS

Hijrah Departure — name given to Muhammad's journey to Medina.
Idol Statue worshiped as a god.
Meditate To think deeply, especially about religion.
Sacrifice Offering made to a god.

A PRAYER OF MUHAMMAD

My Lord, help me, and do not give help against me; grant me victory and do not grant victory over me. Guide me and make my right guidance easy for me; grant me victory over those who act wrongfully toward me.

O Allah, make me grateful to you, mindful of you, full of reverence toward you, devoted to your obedience, humble before you and penitent. My Lord, accept my repentance, wash away my sin, answer my prayer, establish my evidence clearly, guide my heart, make true my tongue, and draw out malice from my breast.

Hadith Abu Dawud

THE KORAN

This section tells you about the Koran, the Muslims' holy book.

Muslims believe that the words of the Koran are the words of Allah. They were given to Muhammad by the Angel Gabriel. The word Koran means **recitation**, and Muslims believe that Muhammad recited what the Angel Gabriel taught him. He then taught several of his friends, and they too learned the words by heart. Muhammad could not read or write, but the friends who had learned it wrote it down. The Koran was written down in one book within 20 years of Muhammad's death.

Muslims believe that the words of the Koran should not be changed in any way, because they are the words of Allah. Muslims who do not speak Arabic may have a translation into their own language for their own use, but for worship the Koran is always read in Arabic. All Muslims can recite parts of the Koran in Arabic.

Copies of the Koran are treated with great respect. When a copy is not being used, it is kept carefully wrapped on the highest piece of furniture in the room. Before reading it, a Muslim will wash, or sometimes have a bath. The Koran is often placed on a stand to be read, so that it does not have to be handled too much. Some Muslims learn the whole of the Koran by heart, because they believe that what it teaches is so important. Those who succeed in doing this are allowed to use the title **hafiz** as part of their name.

Contents of the Koran

The Koran is made up of 114 chapters, which are called **surahs**. These are of different lengths. The longest is surah 2, which has 286 verses, the shortest is surah 103, which has only three verses. Except for surah 9, they all begin with the words "In the name of Allah, most gra-

This girl is reading the Koran.

cious, most merciful." Some surahs describe events, others offer teaching. The teaching is very detailed, and Muslims believe that it is important because it tells them how they should live.

The Koran does not say that Muhammad was Allah's only prophet. It accepts that people who are important in the teachings of **Judaism** and **Christianity** were prophets, too. For example, Abraham (Muslims call him Ibrahim), Moses (Musa), and Jesus (Isa) are all mentioned in the Koran. According to the Koran, the problem was that even though they had the teachings of these prophets, people kept forgetting what Allah was like. Allah called Muhammad to be his prophet and gave him the Koran so that people would not forget his teachings. Muslims believe that the **scriptures** of other religions were given by God, but they have been altered by human beings. Only the Koran has been kept in its original form and so is truly the word of Allah. In other words, Muslims believe that Islam completes what Judaism and Christianity began.

The Hadith

For Muslims, the **Hadith** is the other important collection of teachings. The books of the Hadith contain the collected sayings of Muhammad.

This is the first surah in a decorated copy of the Koran.

They are still used today to advise Muslims on how to act. A Muslim with a problem—not just in their faith, but in any area of their life—will look in the Hadith to find out what Muhammad said or did in the same or a similar situation.

THE NATURE OF ALLAH

This passage from the Koran shows what Islam teaches about the nature of Allah.

> *Allah! There is no god*
>
> *But he, — the living,*
>
> *The self-subsisting, eternal,*
>
> *No slumber can seize him,*
>
> *Nor sleep. His are all things*
>
> *In the heavens and on earth ...*
>
> *His throne extends*
>
> *Over the heavens*
>
> *And the earth, and he feels*
>
> *No fatigue in guarding*
>
> *And preserving them*
>
> *For he is the most high*
>
> *The supreme (in glory).*

Surah 2 : 255

NEW WORDS

Christianity The religion of Christians.
Hadith Teachings based on the life of Muhammad.
Hafiz A person who has learned the Koran by heart.
Judaism Religion of the Jews.
Recitation Repeating something learned by heart.
Scriptures Holy books.
Surah Chapter in the Koran.

THE MOSQUE

This section tells you about the place where Muslims go to worship.

Muslims believe that they can worship Allah anywhere, and they do not have to be in a special building. However, like members of most other religions, many Muslims feel that it is important to have a special place for worship. This place is called a mosque. (The Arabic name *masjid* is sometimes used instead.) Many Muslim men go to the mosque several times a week, but the most important time is the lunchtime prayers on a Friday, the Muslim holy day. Women are expected to pray too, either at the mosque or at home. When they go to the mosque, they stay separate from the men. Muslims believe that this allows both men and women to concentrate on Allah.

A mosque usually has a **dome** and at least one tall tower called a **minaret**. From the top of this tower, the **adhan** is called five times a day. This is the call to prayer, and many mosques have loudspeakers so that the adhan can be heard clearly.

An essential part of all mosques is a supply of water. Sometimes this is in a courtyard with a pool or fountain; sometimes it is in a cloakroom. It is needed because all Muslims wash before they pray. This is a special washing, explained on page 16, which has nothing to do with being dirty. Muslims also take off their shoes before they go into the mosque, to show respect and to keep the mosque clean for prayer.

Inside a mosque

Many mosques are beautifully decorated. There are never any pictures or statues, because Muhammad said that these should be avoided in case people began to worship them. The decorations are made with cleverly designed patterns and verses from the Koran. Often the verses are made into patterns, too.

There are no seats in a mosque, but the floor is carpeted or has special prayer mats. When they pray, Muslims always face Mecca, so mosques have a small arch in one wall that shows the exact direction of Mecca. This is called the **mihrab**. There is also a raised platform that is usually at the top of a short flight of steps. This is called the **minbar**. It is used by the **imam** when he preaches on a Friday. The imam is a leader who is chosen by other Muslims because he knows the Koran well. Being an imam is not always the man's full-time job, and he is not always paid. Preaching in a mosque is based on the Koran. The imam explains its teachings and talks about life as a Muslim.

A large mosque in a Western city.

Notice the mihrab in the front of this mosque.

Mosques are used for prayers every day, and they are also used for other things that have to do with the religion. For example, in the United States, Muslim children go to the mosque after school to learn about Islam and the Koran, because they are not taught much about them at school.

NEW WORDS

Adhan The call to prayer.
Dome Roof shaped like half a ball.
Imam Muslim leader and teacher.
Mihrab The arch in the wall that shows the direction of Mecca.
Minaret Tower of a mosque.
Minbar Platform used for preaching.

ALLAH AS LIGHT

This is part of the "parable of the light" which is often used in Muslim worship.

Allah is the light

Of the heavens and the earth ...

(Lit is such a light)

In houses which Allah

Has permitted to be raised

To honor; for celebration

In them of his name:

In them is he glorified

In the mornings and

in the evenings (again and again).

Surah 24 : 35–36

THE FIVE PILLARS OF ISLAM

This section tells you about the most important parts of Muslim worship.

There are five most important parts to Muslim worship. They are called the five pillars of Islam. A pillar is something which supports a building, so the five pillars of Islam support the religion. Muslims believe that following the five pillars helps them to keep their religion properly.

The first pillar—Shahadah

Shahadah is the declaration of faith. In other words, it is a summing up of the most important part of Muslim belief. It is usually translated into English as "There is no other god but Allah, and Muhammad is the prophet of Allah."

These words form part of the adhan, the call to prayer. (See page 12). They are whispered into the ear of newborn babies, so that they are the first words they hear. Muslims who are still able to speak will repeat them as they are dying. These are the first words that a Muslim says on waking up, and the last they say before going to sleep.

The second pillar—Salat

Salat means prayer five times a day. Muslims pray early in the morning, at night, and on three occasions during the day. Male Muslims are expected to go to the mosque for the noon prayers on a Friday, but otherwise they pray in any clean place. When it is time for prayer, Muslims stop whatever they are doing and face in the direction of Mecca. (The positions for prayers are described on pages 16–17.) In Muslim countries, a **mu'adhin** calls the people to prayer from the mosque. (Mu'adhin is sometimes written "muezzin.") He recites the adhan, and adds, "Come to prayer, come to security, Allah is most great!" In the morning, he adds the words "Prayer is better than sleep!"

The third pillar—Zakah

Zakah means giving money to people who are poor or in need. Every year, Muslims are expected to give a certain amount of their money to charity. This can be used for things like building hospitals as well as direct help for poorer Muslims. This money is called Zakah or sometimes Zakat. It amounts to about 2.5 percent of the money that a Muslim has received and not

The five pillars.

FAITH   PRAYER   ALMS   FASTING   PILGRIMAGE

14

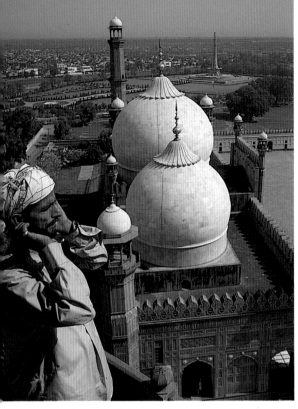

A mu'adhin making the call to prayer.

NEW WORDS

Fasting Doing without food and drink for religious reasons.
Mu'adhin A man who calls Muslims to prayer.
Pilgrimage Journey for religious reasons.

THE CALL TO PRAYER

Allahu-Akbar ...

God is the Greatest,
God is the Greatest,
God is the Greatest,
God is the Greatest,
I bear witness that there is no
God but Allah,
I bear witness that there is no
God but Allah,
I bear witness that Muhammad
is the messenger of Allah,
I bear witness that Muhammad
is the messenger of Allah,
Come to prayer,
Come to prayer,
Come to security,
Come to security,
God is the most great,
God is the most great,
There is no God but Allah.

spent in a year. It does not include money that is spent on necessary things like food and clothes. Zakah is thought of as being an offering to Allah, so all Muslims are expected to give it. Not to give Zakah would mean that they were not doing their duty to poorer Muslims, and — even more important — it would mean that they were cheating Allah.

The fourth pillar—Sawm

Sawm is **fasting** during the month of Ramadan. Ramadan is the ninth month of the Muslim year. During this month, most Muslims do not eat or drink during the hours of daylight. They try hard to live especially good lives. (This is explained in more detail on page 22.)

The fifth pillar—Hajj

Hajj is **pilgrimage** to Mecca. Every Muslim who can afford it is expected to visit Mecca at least once during their life. For Muslims, Mecca is a most holy place, because it is where Muhammad lived and worked. (Hajj is explained in more detail on pages 18–21.)

MUSLIM WORSHIP

This section tells you about how Muslims worship.

The most important part of Muslim worship is prayer. Prayer five times a day is the second of the five pillars of Islam. Muslims always pray facing toward Mecca. In a mosque, there is a special arch in the wall to show the direction to face. For prayers when they are not in a mosque, Muslims can carry a special compass. Using this, they can work out the position of Mecca from anywhere in the world. If the floor is not clean, Muslims use a special mat for prayers. After the set prayers, Muslims may use a string of 33 or 99 beads to allow them to remember Allah 99 times. There are 99 names for Allah in the Koran — the wise, the merciful, etc. Some Muslims count with the finger joints of their right hand instead of using beads.

The times of prayers are laid down in the Koran. The first prayers should be between first light and sunrise, the second after the sun has left the highest point in the sky. The third prayers should be between midafternoon and sunset, the fourth between sunset and darkness. The fifth prayers of the day are between darkness and first light. In Muslim countries, the people are reminded that it is time to pray by the mu'adhin who calls them to prayer from the mosque.

Wudu

Before praying, Muslims wash. This is a special washing, called **wudu**, and has nothing to do with being dirty. If they are actually dirty, Muslims bath completely before praying. Wudu is intended to make the person fit to worship Allah, who is holy. It gives them time to forget what they were doing, and get ready to concentrate on Allah. Some Muslims prefer to use cold water for washing, so that they are more alert, especially at the morning prayers.

Washing is always done in the same order, to make sure that nothing is forgotten. The instructions for how it should be done are in the Koran. First, the right hand is washed, to the wrist. Then, the left hand in the same way. Next, the mouth and throat, by gargling, so that the voice is clean to talk to Allah. Then, the nose and face are washed, and the right arm up to the elbow, then the left. The head is wiped with a wet hand, then the ears are cleaned. Finally, the feet are washed up to the ankles, right one first. If no water is available, clean sand or earth may be used instead.

Rak'ahs

When a Muslim prays, they do not just make up prayers, although there is opportunity for private prayer. The prayers follow a set pattern called a **rak'ah**. Two rak'ahs are made at morning prayers, four at midday and in the afternoon, three in the evening, and four at night.

A rak'ah includes several different positions. The Muslim stands, bows, kneels, and touches the ground with the forehead. Different parts of the prayer are said in each position.

Wudu is the special washing before prayer.

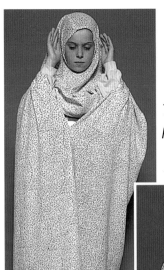

The first prayer position.

The position for making personal prayers.

NEW WORDS

Du'a Personal prayers.
Rak'ah A set of positions for Muslim prayers.
Wudu Special washing before prayer.

INSTRUCTIONS FOR WUDU

This is part of a longer set of instructions about how to perform the special washing before prayer.

> *O you who believe!*
>
> *When you prepare*
>
> *For prayer, wash*
>
> *Your faces, and your hands*
>
> *(And arms) to the elbows;*
>
> *Rub your heads (with water);*
>
> *And (wash) your feet*
>
> *To the ankles...*
>
> *Allah does not wish*
>
> *To place you in a difficulty,*
>
> *But to make you clean,*
>
> *And to complete*
>
> *His favor to you,*
>
> *That you may be grateful.*

Surah 5 : 6

The following description is of a man praying, but women pray in the same way.

The first movement shows that he intends to pray. In the second, he repeats the first verses of the Koran ("You alone do we worship . . . .") In positions three to eight, he praises Allah for his goodness. In the ninth movement, he prays for Muhammad and all Muslims everywhere. He turns his head from side to side, to greet the two angels whom Muslims believe are always with every person, though they cannot be seen.

At the end of the set prayer, the Muslim can add his own private prayers if he wishes. These are called **du'a**. He stays in a kneeling position, with his hands palm upwards. Some Muslims wipe their hand over their face as a sign that they have finished their prayers. Du'a can be made at any time, in addition to at the end of a rak'ah.

THE HAJJ I

This section tells you about how Muslims prepare for pilgrimage to Mecca.

Hajj, or pilgrimage to Mecca, is the fifth of the five pillars of Islam. Every Muslim who has the health and wealth is expected to go to Mecca at least once during their life. Many people save up for years until they can afford it, and often families join together to pay for one person to go. Every year, about two million Muslims travel from all over the world to make Hajj. For each of them, it is a very special journey, and one that they will remember all their lives.

To be a true Hajj, the pilgrimage must take place between the 8th and the 13th of Dhul-Hijjah, the last month of the Muslim year. Of course, Muslims can go to Mecca at other times, but the pilgrimage is then called **Umrah**, and is not so important. Today, there are so many Muslims wanting to go for Hajj that Muslims who have been before are encouraged to go at other times of the year. Non-Muslims may enter the holy city of Mecca, but not the Ka'bah.

Ihram

Ihram is the word given to the special state in which pilgrims are expected to live while they are on Hajj. They are expected to live pure lives and are not supposed to swear or quarrel. Any sexual relationship is forbidden, even if husbands and wives are together. As a sign of the purity of the thoughts of all pilgrims, women are not allowed to cover their faces, even if they do so in their normal life.

The pilgrim camp.

All male pilgrims wear exactly the same clothes, two sheets of white cotton that do not have any seams. One sheet covers the lower half of their body, the other is worn over the left shoulder. These clothes are also called "ihram." They are worn so that everyone looks alike, and it does not matter whether they are old or young, rich or poor. It is a sign that everyone is equal before Allah. Men may not cover their heads, although they are allowed to carry an umbrella to protect themselves from the heat of the sun. Women do not wear special clothes, but they wear head veils, and make sure that everything they wear is simple. Pilgrims should go barefoot, or wear only open sandals. To add to the simplicity, no one wears jewelry or perfume or uses scented soap. Hair and nails are not trimmed during Hajj.

Men who have completed the Hajj can be called Hajji, women Hajjah. For every pilgrim, Hajj is a very joyful time. They share worship with thousands of other pilgrims, but the point of the Hajj is that for each pilgrim, it is an individual experience.

The purpose of Hajj is to "meet" Allah. Muslims believe that if Hajj is properly performed in the right frame of mind a pilgrim can gain forgiveness for everything he or she has done wrong in his or her life.

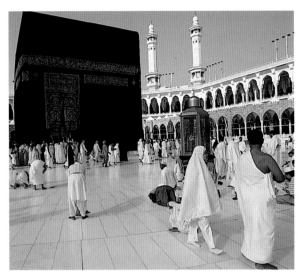

Pilgrims wearing ihram.

CONDITIONS FOR HAJJ

> *For Hajj*
>
> *Are the months well known.*
>
> *If anyone undertakes*
>
> *The duty therein,*
>
> *Let there be no obscenity*
>
> *Nor wickedness,*
>
> *Not wrangling*
>
> *In the Hajj.*
>
> *And whatever good*
>
> *You do, (be sure)*
>
> *That Allah knows it.*
>
> *Surah 2 : 197*

NEW WORDS

Hajj Pilgrimage to Mecca.
Ihram Special way of living for Hajj. (Also the special clothes).
Umrah "Lesser pilgrimage."

THE HAJJ II

This section tells you about how Muslims perform the Hajj.

Most pilgrims sail or fly to start the pilgrimage at Jeddah, then travel on to Mecca by bus or car. When they reach Mecca, they go first to the Great Mosque which contains the **Ka'bah.**

The Ka'bah is a cube-shaped building 49 feet (15 m) long, 33 feet (10 m) wide, and 46 feet (14 m) high. Inside it is a room that is decorated with parts of the Koran. Muslims believe that the Ka'bah is the oldest place of worship of Allah, since it was built by Ibrahim and his son Isma'il, forefathers of the Arab people. It is covered by a black cloth that is embroidered with the words of the Koran. This cloth is replaced every year because, at the end of each Hajj, pieces are given to some pilgrims, perhaps kings or diplomats, as a reminder of the pilgrimage. In one corner is the black stone. Muslims believe that this was given to Ibrahim's son, Isma'il, by the Angel Gabriel. Every pilgrim walks or runs around the Ka'bah seven times. Those who are close enough touch it or kiss it. Those farther away raise their hands toward it.

Pilgrims walk round the Ka'bah.

After they have done this, the pilgrims go to pray near the Maqam Ibrahim (Ibrahim's place), which is close to the Ka'bah. Then they hurry seven times between two small hills not far from the Ka'bah. This reminds believers how Ibrahim's wife Hajar ran between these two hills looking for water for her baby son Isma'il. Today the hills are linked by a broad corridor. The spring that Muslims believe Isma'il found when he dug his toes in the sand is now called the Well of Zamzam, and is in the courtyard of the Great Mosque. Pilgrims drink water from this well and often take some home for family and friends.

The ninth day of the month is usually the second or third day of the pilgrimage, and the pilgrims travel to the Plain of Arafat, which is about 12 miles (20 km) from Mecca. They travel there to "stand before Allah"—**wuquf.** They ask Allah to forgive all their **sins,** the wrong things that they have done in their life. The pilgrims stand from midday until sunset, thinking about Allah and praying. This is the most important part of the pilgrimage, and without it the Hajj is not complete. Then they travel back to Muzdalifah in time for the evening prayers and camp there overnight.

The corridor that links the two hills.

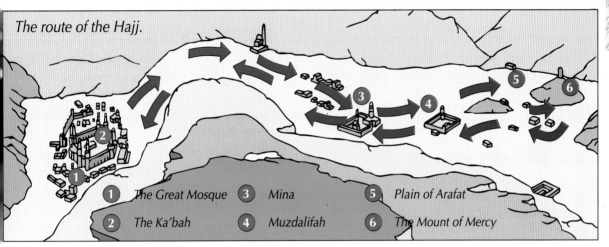

The route of the Hajj.

| 1 | The Great Mosque | 3 | Mina | 5 | Plain of Arafat |
| 2 | The Ka'bah | 4 | Muzdalifah | 6 | The Mount of Mercy |

On the morning of the tenth day, the pilgrims go to Mina, where there are three stone pillars. Pilgrims throw stones at these seven times, to recall how Ibrahim and his family drove away the **Devil** who was tempting them. After the first pillar has been stoned, many pilgrims sacrifice an animal, usually a sheep or a goat. This is part of the festival of Id ul Adha, which is celebrated by Muslims all over the world. Male pilgrims then either shave their heads or cut their hair, and women cut off a lock of their hair. They do this because it is what Muhammad did. Then they take off the special pilgrim clothes and put on their normal clothes. The pilgrims camp at Mina for three days, after which they travel back to Mecca and walk around the Ka'bah again. They drink as much water as they can from the Well of Zamzam. Then the Hajj is ended, and the pilgrims can travel home if they wish. In fact, many choose to stay and visit other important places in the area—for example, the Mosque of the Prophet and Muhammad's tomb at Medina.

NEW WORDS

Devil Spirit of evil.
Ka'bah Most important place of Muslim worship.
Sins Wrongdoing — something which separates a person from God.
Wuquf "Stand before Allah" — the most important part of Hajj.

PRAYER SAID BY PILGRIMS ENTERING MECCA

O God,

this sanctuary is your sacred place,

and this city is your city,

and this slave is your slave.

I have come to you from a distant land,

carrying all my sins and misdeeds

as an afflicted person seeking your help

and dreading your punishment.

I beg you to accept me,

and grant me your complete forgiveness,

and give me permission to enter

your vast garden of delight.

RAMADAN

This section tells you about an important Muslim celebration.

Every year, during the month called Ramadan, Muslims fast during the hours of daylight. The custom of fasting in Ramadan goes back to the time of Muhammad. He taught his followers that the fast was important, because it was a sign that they had submitted to Allah. Fasting like this is very hard, but Muslims believe that it teaches them to have patience and not to give up just because things are difficult. It also reminds them that their religion is the most important thing in their lives, far more important than food and drink. One of the aims of Ramadan is to make everyone equal because hunger is the same for everyone, whether they are rich or poor. At the end of a successful Ramadan, a Muslim feels much more able to face up to any problems that life brings.

Prayers at a mosque in Istanbul.

During Ramadan, all eating must finish before dawn, so the day begins well before this. To make sure that there is no confusion about what time fasting should begin or end, special lists are published showing the times of dawn and sunset in different places. The first meal is not usually a large one, but it contains foods that will give energy for the day. Then the Muslim's life goes on as normal, except that they eat and drink nothing. At sunset, they have a light snack, followed later by a main meal.

It is very difficult to eat and drink nothing all day, especially in hot countries. Sometimes it may become too much, and a person may feel that he or she must eat or drink. If a Muslim breaks the fast without a good reason, he or she should fast for one extra day. Ramadan is intended to be difficult, but it is not intended to be cruel. Therefore exceptions are made, and not all Muslims are expected to fast. The very old and the young, children who have not reached maturity, are excused. People who are on a journey may eat while they are traveling, but should make up the extra days of fasting later. Anyone who is ill is not expected to fast, and neither is a woman who is pregnant. They are expected to make up the missed days when they are healthy. If someone has a health problem that means they can never fast, they are expected to pay a sum of money which would buy a meal for 60 people.

Although these things are expected of Muslims, whether or not they do them is up to each individual's conscience. There are no punishments if they do not keep the fast. Muslims believe that the judge of someone's behavior is Allah, who knows everything and sees everything. At the end of the world, Allah will judge everyone on how they have lived, and each person will get what he or she deserves. The point is that if they fail to do what their religion expects, they

A Muslim family in Europe breaking their fast.

NEW WORDS

Day of Judgment The end of the world, when Allah will judge everyone.
Retreat A special time of praying and thinking.

INSTRUCTIONS FOR RAMADAN

are cheating not only themselves, but Allah, too. Muhammad taught that everyone who fasts will get two rewards. They will get the joy of being able to eat again when the fast has finished, and they will also be rewarded by Allah at the **Day of Judgment.**

As well as fasting, Muslims try to live especially pure lives during Ramadan. They do not smoke or have sexual relationships during the day. They spend extra time on religious matters. They are expected to attend special prayers, and they spend more time reading the Koran. Many Muslims try to read all the way through the Koran during the month. Some Muslims choose to go and stay in the mosque during the last ten days of Ramadan. This is called a **retreat**. They take only a few necessary possessions with them and live simply, reading the Koran and praying and thinking about spiritual matters. They do this because it is how Muhammad spent the last part of Ramadan when he was alive, so they believe that they are following his example. The month of Ramadan ends with the festival of Id-ul-Fitr.

Ramadan is the (month)

In which was sent down

The Koran, as a guide

To mankind...

So everyone of you

Who is present (at his home)

During that month

Should spend it in fasting.

But if anyone is ill

Or on a journey,

The prescribed period

(Should be made up)

By days later.

Allah intends every facility

For you, he does not want

To put you to [through] *difficulties.*

Surah 2 : 185

Id-ul-Fitr and Id-ul-Adha

This section tells you about two important Muslim festivals.

Id-ul-Fitr

Id-ul-Fitr is the festival which ends Ramadan. It begins on the first day of the tenth month of the Muslim year. It marks the end of the difficult month of fasting, so it is looked forward to very much. Before the festival begins, Muslims observe Zakat-ul-Fitr. This means giving money for the poor. Usually the amount given is what it costs to buy a meal for a family. The idea is that everyone should have enough money to celebrate the feast, no matter how poor they are.

On the last night of Ramadan, many people do not bother to go to bed. Instead, they meet outside to watch for the new moon. When the moon can be seen, the new month of Shawwal has begun, and so the festival can start.

Id cards.

Gifts for Id.

The first day of the festival begins with a light meal. Then Muslims meet at the mosque. Id-ul-Fitr is a time for meeting friends and relatives, so it is common for large groups to meet at the mosque for prayers. The special prayers take place between dawn and noon, and Muslims give thanks for a successful fast. After the prayers, families and friends meet in each other's homes. Id is a time when people who have not seen each other for a long time can meet and talk. There are parties, especially for children, and people give each other presents. Children often wear new clothes. Everyone enjoys special cakes and sweet desserts. Many Muslims also celebrate Id by sending greeting cards to each other. A common greeting is "Id mubarak"—"Id blessings!"

Id-ul-Adha

The festival of Id-ul-Adha takes place in the month of Dhul-Hijjah. It is celebrated by Muslims all over the world, although it is especially important for Muslims who are on the Hajj, the pilgrimage to Mecca. They celebrate the festival at Mina.

The name Id-ul-Adha means Feast of Sacrifice. It is the festival at which Muslims remember that Ibrahim was ready to make a sacrifice of his son, Isma'il. He did not have to do this because, just in time, he heard a voice telling him that he should sacrifice a ram instead. However, the point of the story is that Ibrahim was ready to give up the most important thing in his life, his son, because he believed it was what Allah wanted.

On the morning of the tenth day of Dhul-Hijjah, Muslims may sacrifice an animal. Usually this is a sheep or a goat, though other larger animals are sometimes used, especially if families join together to make the sacrifice. Sacrificing the animal is a symbol. Its life is being given to Allah, and this is a sign that Muslims themselves are ready to give up everything for Allah.

Like any animal that a Muslim is going to eat, the animal sacrificed at Id-ul-Adha is killed in a special way. All the blood is drained away, and it becomes **halal**. "Halal" means allowed, so halal meat is meat which Muslims are allowed to eat. (This is explained in more detail on pages 40–41.) The meat from the sacrificed animal is shared, and one-third of it is always given to the poor.

Like Id-ul-Fitr, Muslims celebrate the rest of the festival with family and friends, and by exchanging presents. Id-ul-Adha is a longer and more important festival than Id-ul-Fitr.

NEW WORD

Halal "Allowed" — food that Muslims can eat.

SWEET VERMICELLI

This is a version of a traditional dish for Id-ul-Fitr.

Ingredients

1 package very fine vermicelli noodles
1 pint milk
1 cup (250g) sugar
5 cardamom seeds (split open at the top)
sultanas or raisins
chopped nuts
fresh or canned fruit pieces
3 tablespoons rose water (optional)
few drops cochineal (optional)

Directions

Place the vermicelli in a saucepan with enough milk to cover it.

Add the sugar, and bring to a boil, stirring until it begins to thicken.

Stir well.

Mix in all the other ingredients, and leave to cool.

THE MINOR CELEBRATIONS

This section tells you about some of the days of celebration in the Muslim year.

The Day of the Hijrah (1 Muharram)

Muharram is the first month of the Muslim year, so the first day of Muharram is New Year's Day in the Muslim calendar. It is also important for another reason. It is the day on which Muslims remember the journey that Muhammad made from Mecca to Medina. They believe that this was a very important event, because it was after this that Islam became important as a religion. Therefore, this day is not just the day which marks the beginning of the new year, it is also the day on which Muslims remember the beginning of the success of Islam. Many Muslims make New Year's resolutions on this day, believing that they are leaving behind their old ways in the same way that Muhammad left Mecca.

The Dome of the Rock mosque in Jerusalem.

The Prophet's birthday (12 Rabi al-Awwal)

Muhammad's birthday was on the 12th day of the third month of the year, which is called Rabi al-Awwal. Some Muslims celebrate this as a special day, because of their love for Muhammad and because they believe he was the last and most important of all the prophets. During this month Muslims may meet to remember events in Muhammad's life. Many Muslims do not agree with attaching this much importance to the birth of a human being, and so do not approve of the celebrations.

The Night of Power (27 Ramadan)

This festival remembers the night when Muhammad first received the Koran from the Angel Gabriel. It falls during the last part of the month of Ramadan. Most Muslims celebrate it on the 27th day of Ramadan, although the exact date on which it occurred is not known. Many Muslims spend extra time reading the Koran at this time, and thinking about its importance in their lives.

The Night of the Journey (27 Rajab)

Muslims believe that on the night of the 27th day of Rajab, Muhammad made an amazing journey from Mecca to Jerusalem. (Some Muslims believe that it was a vision rather than something which really happened.) From Jerusalem, Muhammad was taken up to heaven, and heard Allah telling him to teach his followers about the importance of prayer five times a day. The most important mosque in Jerusalem, the Mosque of the Dome of the Rock, is built at the place from which it is said that Muhammad was taken up to heaven.

The celebrations for the different festivals are not the same, but they are all times when families and friends can get together. This can be very important, especially when people do not live as close to their relatives as they did in the past. Muslims believe strongly that festivals should be times of happiness and friendship where everyone is involved.

THE NIGHT OF POWER

We have indeed revealed

This (message)

In the Night of Power: …

The Night of Power

is better than

A thousand months.

Therein come down

The angels and the Spirit

By Allah's permission

On every errand.

Surah 97 : 1, 3, 4

THE HISTORY OF ISLAM

This section tells you something about the history of Islam.

After Muhammad died, the area of land which Muslims ruled grew quickly. Muhammad had taught that fighting was not wrong if it was to defeat persecution. Trying to overcome any sort of evil is called **jihad**, which means to struggle. It is an important part of Muslim belief. This can mean that fighting battles is permitted, if there is no other way. The men who took over from Muhammad as leaders of Islam fought to make Islam grow stronger. Their first task was to conquer the groups that had left Islam when Muhammad died. When they had done this, groups further away began to attack, but the Muslims defeated them. Within a hundred years they ruled a very large area.

Over the next few hundred years, Muslims came to rule more and more parts of the world. They went east, and much of India became Muslim. Muslim leaders were in power there until the middle of the nineteenth century. They went west, through the north of Africa, and crossed the Mediterranean Sea into Spain. They went north and, over several hundred years, gained power in a large part of Eastern Europe.

One of the areas where most battles were fought was the land at the eastern end of the Mediterranean Sea. This was the area called Palestine. It is important to Muslims, but it is also important to Jews and to Christians. Jewish and Christian soldiers fought Muslim soldiers over the land for many years. At this time in the Middle Ages holy wars known as the Crusades were fought. Many battles were fought around the city of Jerusalem, because all three religions believe that this is a holy city, and all three wanted to control it. The Muslims were generally better fighters. Where they took control, they allowed the Christians and Jews to continue to follow their own religions, but they had to pay a special tax. This was instead of serving in the Muslim army, which people who had been conquered would normally have been expected to do.

Muslim rule in 732 CE.

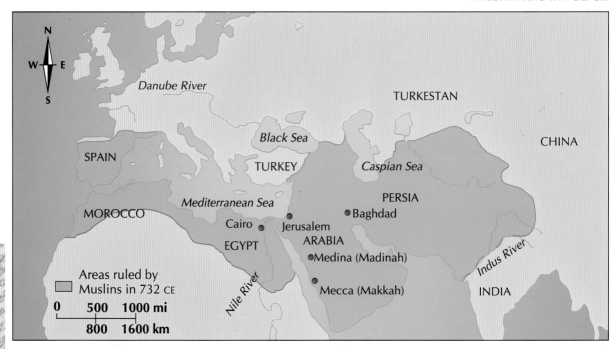

The Alhambra in Spain was built by Muslims.

One of the most important Muslim nations was called the Ottoman Empire. It was most powerful between about 1400 CE and 1600 CE. After this time it lost some of its land, but it did not end until after World War I in 1918. One of its most famous rulers was Süleyman the Magnificent, who ruled from 1520 to 1566.

Islam did not just spread by fighting. Many Muslims were traders, and they traveled all over the world buying and selling goods. Where they traveled, they took their religion with them. They became well known for the fact that they lived good lives, and people respected them. Sometimes the people they met were so impressed that they decided they would become Muslims too, and gradually Islam spread.

Today, there are about one billion followers of Islam, and there are Muslims living in most countries of the world. About 3 million Muslims live in the United States. Islam is growing faster than any other religion.

NEW WORD

Jihad A struggle against evil.

THE OTTOMAN ARMY

This description of the Ottoman army was written in the sixteenth century. It compares the Muslim soldiers with the Christian soldiers they were fighting.

They are ready for fighting. They are used to hard work. Our side is weakened, spirits broken, not enough training. Our soldiers do not obey orders, our officers are greedy and there is drunkenness. Worst of all, they are used to winning, and we are used to losing.

The Turks take care to keep their soldiers in good health and protect them from the weather. There is no quarreling or violence of any kind. You never see any drinking or gambling, which is such a serious problem among our soldiers.

Ogier de Busbecq,
Austrian Ambassador to Istanbul, 1554–62

MODERN ISLAM

This section tells you about the two main groups of Muslims today.

Muhammad and his followers were called Muslims because they had submitted to the will of Allah. While Muhammad was alive, he had the greatest authority among his friends. If there were any arguments, they would ask Muhammad for his advice, and he would help solve the problem. After Muhammad died, his friends decided that they needed a new leader. They decided that the "best" Muslim should be chosen. They agreed that this man was Abu Bakr. Abu Bakr had been one of Muhammad's closest friends. Now he became an important leader called a **khalifah**. After Abu Bakr, three other khalifahs led the Muslims in turn. They were Umar, Uthman, and Ali. Ali was married to Muhammad's daughter. These khalifahs were all chosen by the rest of the group.

About 50 years after Muhammad had died, some Muslims came to have different opinions about how khalifahs should be chosen. They began to feel that rather than being chosen by other Muslims, khalifahs should be members of Muhammad's family. Muhammad's sons had died when they were children, so they believed the first khalifah should have been Ali, Muhammad's son-in-law. The next should have been Ali's son, and so on. The disagreement became more and more bitter, until the Muslims who supported Ali's family split away into a separate group. They are called Shi'ah Muslims. About ten percent of Muslims in the world today belong to this group.

Shi'ah Muslims

Most Shi'ah Muslims live in Iran and Iraq. Many Shi'ahs are very strict about what they believe and are often more extreme in their views. It is part of Muslim belief that anyone who is a **martyr** will go straight to Allah and live in **Paradise**. A martyr is someone who dies for their faith. The fact that they believe this means that Muslims are sometimes ready to give up their life in fighting for what they believe is right. This is one reason why Shi'ah Muslims are often in the news.

Countries where over 50 percent of the people are Muslim.

Shi'ah Muslims.

Muslims believe that they need teachers to help them understand what the Koran means. All Muslim teachers are called "imams," but Shi'ahs believe that there were 12 imams who were given special power by Allah, just as Muhammad was. They believe that the first imam was Ali, who was chosen by Muhammad. His power was passed on from father to son until the last imam, who disappeared in 880 CE. Shi'ahs believe that he will return one day and, until he does, his teachings are in the hands of doctors of the law. The most important of these leaders are called **Ayatollahs**.

Sunni Muslims

When the Shi'ahs split away, a much bigger group of Muslims was left behind. This group became the Sunni Muslims. The word "Sunni" comes from an Arabic word meaning

NEW WORDS

Ayatollah Leader of Shi'ah Muslims.
Khalifah Early leader of Islam.
Martyr Someone who dies for their faith.
Paradise Garden of happiness for life after death.

authority. Sunnis think of themselves as the true followers of Muhammad's teachings. Today about 90 percent of Muslims belong to the Sunnis. The main difference between Sunni and Shi'ah belief is that the Sunnis accept the first four khalifahs as the true leaders of Islam, but Shi'ahs only accept Ali and his sons. They also have different opinions about what some parts of the Koran mean. Over many years, Sunnis and Shi'ahs gradually developed laws to make sure that the teachings of the Koran were followed. These laws have become the national laws for Muslim countries.

PRAYER FOR FORGIVENESS

This is part of a prayer for forgiveness from a book used in the Sudan.

> *I ask for forgiveness for myself and for all Muslims, both men and women; for all believers, both men and women; for those of them who are alive and those of them who are dead. Deal with me and with them, whether soon or late, in the faith, in this world and the next, according to what you deserve. Do not deal with us, O Lord, according to what we deserve. For you are forgiving, patient, generous, bountiful, tender, and merciful. We pray you to turn our desires toward you. For you alone can rescue us from danger in this world and the next.*

From a book of prayers used by Imam Muhammad al Mahdi

ISLAM'S INFLUENCE

This section tells you about some of the ways that Islam has changed the world.

Muhammad taught his friends that it was important to make the most of what Allah has given, so Muslims have always been interested in the world around them. Muslim leaders have always encouraged their people to explore areas such as science and art, and this has led to many inventions and discoveries. Hundreds of years ago, great universities and libraries were built in many Muslim cities and became centers of learning where scholars from many countries went to study. About 1000 CE, for example, there was a large library attached to the palace in Cairo in Egypt. Ordinary people were not only allowed to use it free of charge, but also provided with ink, pens, and paper.

Medicine

Muslim doctors were the first to believe that blood circulated around the body, and they invented the first ways of treating some very serious diseases. They discovered that plants — especially herbs — could be used to treat people who were ill. They were the first to find a way of putting patients to sleep for operations. These discoveries were so important that their ideas were followed by other people for hundreds of years. A famous Muslim doctor was Al-Razi, who lived in Baghdad from 850 CE to 932 CE. He wrote many books and is the first person ever known to have written about diseases in children.

Mathematics

Muslims were very interested in the science of numbers — mathematics — and the study of the stars which is called astronomy. One reason for this was that it was important to be able to work out the position of Mecca for prayer and to be able to work out the right time for prayers. The Arabic system of numbering (1, 2, 3, etc.) came first from Muslims, and early Muslims invented a calendar that is as accurate as any in use today. Algebra was developed by Muslim mathematicians.

Social developments

One of the sayings of Muhammad was "Cleanliness is half of faith." Muslim rulers went to great lengths to make sure that their people had clean water to drink and wash in. In the tenth century CE, most towns in Europe were poor, crowded, and dirty. Water came from the same stream or river where rubbish was thrown. In Muslim countries at the same time, there were houses with running water and drains, and towns were well planned with streets, schools, and public libraries. Some towns even had streetlamps that were lit at night. It was hundreds of years before people in Europe began to copy these ideas.

Muslims were the inventors of a new way of building that meant arches could become much slimmer and more pointed.

This compass and sundial was made in the sixteenth century CE.

Islamic buildings are often very beautiful.

This was copied by European builders and used in many buildings that are still admired for their beauty. Muslims were also responsible for many other things that we all still use today. They brought paper to Europe, and their names for many products have become English words — "apricot," "sugar," and "coffee" all started as Arabic words, and so did "alcohol," "jacket," and "mattress."

Islam's effect on the world can never be measured. Many people who have little idea about the religion use ideas and words which were first thought of by Muslims. This is a reminder that Islam is not just a religion, it is also a way of life which goes back hundreds of years.

A MUSLIM CITY

Today, Baghdad is the capital of the country called Iraq. At the beginning of the ninth century CE it was the largest city on earth. This is what it was like:

> *Baghdad was founded in 762 CE and completed in 766 CE. It was built by 100,000 workers. It was perfectly round, built in concentric circles, each one inside the next. It had four gates and 360 towers. On the outside was a ditch 66 feet (20 m) wide, and a wall 30 feet (9 m) thick. The main wall was over 98 feet (30 m) high and 46 feet (14 m) wide at the top. One section was reserved for the government and the army, and was closed off by a wall 57 feet (17.5 m) high and 66 feet (20 m) thick. At the center of the city was a huge square. Here stood the Golden Palace which had a copper dome, and the Great Mosque. No one entered this central space except on foot and with orders to do so.*

Cambridge Illustrated History of the Middle Ages, Volume 1

ISLAMIC ART

This section tells you something about art in Islam.

Why is Islamic art special?

The kind of art and decorations that Muslims use are quite special. One reason for this is that Muhammad told his friends not to draw pictures of animals or people. Only Allah can make living things, and it is wrong for human beings to try to imitate this. Muhammad was also afraid that if they made pictures or statues, they might begin to worship them. This would be idol-worship, and the Koran teaches that the worship of idols is totally wrong. This is because it is wrong to worship anything which is not perfect. Only Allah is perfect, therefore, only Allah should be worshiped. Instead of pictures of living creatures, Muslim artists tend to concentrate on beautiful drawings of flowers and plants, and especially, decorations using lines and patterns.

Some of the most beautiful examples of pattern-making are in cloths and material. It is easy to understand this by looking back at the lives of early Muslims. In the area of the world where Islam began, many of the people were **nomads,** who spent their lives moving from place to place. Where land is almost desert, they had to travel to find grass for the animals. Rugs and cushions were often used instead of chairs and beds because they are easier to carry around. Many nomads became skilled weavers of cloth. Part of their skill was making cloth attractive to look at, and many traditional patterns developed.

Anything woven by a Muslim always has a deliberate mistake. This is to avoid the weaving's being perfect because Muslims believe that only Allah can make something that is perfect. Many people who were not Muslims found the rugs and cloth attractive, too, so they became

These two photographs show how patterns are used to make beautiful decorations on buildings.

important for trading. This trading is one of the ways in which Islam spread.

Calligraphy

Calligraphy is a special form of decoration. It is the name given to writing which is done so beautifully that it becomes a pattern in itself. It began when Muslims began copying the Koran. To write the words was considered to be a great honor, and Muslims wanted to write them as beautifully as possible. Muslim calligraphers often use quotations from the Koran, or from the sayings of Muhammad. The name of Allah is a favorite word to making patterns from. Writing out words and sayings like this is a way of reminding Muslims how important the words are. Many copies of the Koran are still handwritten today, for this reason.

Calligraphy is often used instead of pictures because of Muhammad's teaching about not drawing living things. Patterns are used on pottery, tiles, bowls, and plates in addition to embroidery and weaving. Decorations like this are

often used in mosques, but they can also be seen in Muslims' homes and in other Islamic buildings. Calligraphy can also be found in the beautiful jewelry worn by Muslim women.

NEW WORDS

Calligraphy   The art of beautiful writing.

TEACHING ABOUT PICTURES

The Hadith is the collection of teaching that comes from Muhammad's life and things he said when he was alive. This part of the Hadith tells what happened when Muhammad's wife hung a curtain with pictures on it in the doorway.

> *Angels will not enter a house containing a dog or statues. Aisha [Muhammad's wife] bought a door curtain on which there were pictures. When Muhammad saw it he stood at the door and would not enter. They took down the curtain, cut it up, and made it into cushions. Muhammad disliked the curtain because he said that the pictures distracted him from his prayers.*

From the Hadith Muslim.

Calligraphy.
This is part of Sura 112 in the Koran.

THE MUSLIM FAMILY

This section tells you something about Muslim families.

The Ummah

Muslims regard all followers of Islam as being members of one big family. This is called the **Ummah**. The idea of the Ummah is very important and helps to explain why Muslims are so concerned about other Muslims wherever they live in the world. Although it is not always the case, many Muslims feel that the fact that someone else is a follower of Islam is far more important than what country they happen to come from, or where they live.

A Muslim family.

Family life

The Koran says that the idea of family life comes from Allah. Playing your part in keeping your home secure and happy is seen as an important part of being a Muslim.

The Western idea of a family's being just parents and children is one which Muslims do not share, and most Muslims live in **extended families** where grandparents, uncles, aunts, and others live either together or close by. Family ties are often very strong, and quite distant relatives can be thought of as "cousins." Children are seen as being a great blessing from Allah, so having many children is a way of showing Allah's goodness.

Grandparents are important members of the family.

Every member of a family has duties toward other members of the family. The parents' duties to their children begin with choosing a suitable name for the child. These duties continue as the children grow up, and include the responsibility of helping to choose a suitable partner for their marriage. Islam also teaches very firmly that children have duties to their parents. Elderly relatives are treated with great respect because it is felt that their experience of life makes them wise. The Western idea of nursing homes for the elderly is one that many Muslims find quite shocking. Islam teaches that it is the duty of children to care for their parents when they are old. Muslims believe that the place for elderly people is with the rest of the family, where they can be loved and cared for in the same way that they loved and cared for their children when they were younger. Grandparents are always seen as the head of the family.

Muslim families live together in a very open way, but family life is private. Many Muslim homes have a special guest room where male visitors can be entertained by the men. Female visitors usually stay with the women. Men and women of the family usually eat together, but when there are guests, visiting women usually eat with the women of the family.

ATTITUDE TO PARENTS

This passage from the Koran shows how Islam teaches that parents should be respected.

> *Your Lord has decreed*
>
> *That you worship none but him,*
>
> *And that you be kind*
>
> *To parents. Whether one*
>
> *Or both of them reach*
>
> *Old age in your life,*
>
> *Say to them not a word*
>
> *Of contempt, nor repel them*
>
> *But address them in terms of honor.*

Surah 17 : 23

WOMEN IN ISLAM

This section tells you something about women in Islam.

At the time of Muhammad, women were treated more or less as servants. They had very few rights and were expected to obey men. Muhammad told Muslims that this was not what Allah wanted, and the teachings of Islam are quite different. The Koran says that women should be respected and cared for, and should have equal rights in education and making decisions. Under the laws of Islam, women are allowed to own things. A woman must be present at any legal ceremony that involves her, unless she chooses to send someone else. To people brought up in Western countries, this is something that would be taken for granted, but in many Eastern countries women are very protected. Male relatives would be expected to act on their behalf.

Marriage

Muslims are expected to marry, and it is normal for the marriage to be **arranged**. This means that a woman's father or male relatives will look into the background and character of a particular man to see if he would be suitable. (A man inquires about a woman who is recommended by his female relatives.) A suitable man would be a Muslim because Muslim law says that children follow the religion of their father, so a non-Muslim father would mean that the children were not Muslim, either. Muslim law says that a woman cannot be forced to marry against her wishes. When she marries, a Muslim woman does not take her husband's family name. Any money or property that she owns before the marriage remains hers. So does any money that she earns if she goes out to work after the marriage. She does not have to give it to her husband unless she wants to.

Work

It is becoming more common for Muslim women to work outside the home, especially since more Muslim women than before are going on to higher education. However, many Muslim women feel that their most important

A Muslim woman doctor.

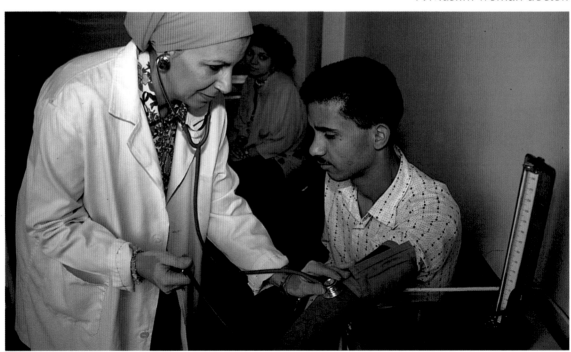

Dressing modestly and covering the head is important for Muslim women.

job is to create a loving home for their husband and family. The family is very important to Muslims, and husbands and wives are seen as having different—but equally important—jobs to do. It is the man's job to go out and earn money that the family needs, and it is the woman's job to look after everybody. Muslim women have the right to an extra allowance if they take care of the home.

Clothes

Muslims feel that many Western women dress in ways that are not modest. They feel that wearing short, low-cut, or tight clothing is intended to show off the body and to tempt men. This is seen as being not only unfair to men, but also degrading to women. All Muslim women should dress decently and keep their legs and arms covered. When they are outside or with strangers, many women choose to dress so that as little as possible of their body can be

seen. This includes wearing a full-length dress and a veil or scarf over their head, and is called **hijab**.

Religion

In religion, Muslim women are expected to follow the same teachings as men. However, they are not required to go to the mosque for the Friday prayers, so that they can be at home with their family. If she does not go to the mosque, a Muslim woman is expected to pray at home. When women worship at the mosque, they pray behind the men, or in a separate room if the prayer hall is too small for everyone.

THE ROLE OF WOMEN

This passage from the Koran shows how Islam teaches that men and women are equal.

> For Muslim men and women,
> For believing men and women,
> For devout men and women,
> For true men and women,
> For men and women who are
> Patient and constant, for men
> And women who humble themselves,
> For men and women who give
> In charity, for men and women
> Who fast (and deny themselves),
> For men and women who guard their
>   chastity and
> For men and women who
> Engage much in Allah's praise —
> For them has Allah prepared
> Forgiveness and a great reward.

Surah 33 : 35

NEW WORDS

Arranged marriage Marriage where relatives make inquiries to make sure the partners are suitable.
Hijab "Veil" — used to describe the modest dress worn by women.

Islam in the Home

This section tells you something about how Muslims live at home.

Muslims believe that their religion affects everything they do because they have submitted their lives to Allah. The way they live at home is therefore a very important part of following their religion. This is probably especially true where they are living in a country where most people are not Muslims, because when children are not taught much about Islam at school, they will learn most of what they know from home. It is also one reason why women are thought of as being so important in Islam. It is usually the mother who teaches the children most about the religion as they are growing up.

Most Muslim families have religious pictures on the walls. These are always placed high up as a sign of respect. Pictures that show people are never used because the Koran forbids them. Reading the Koran together is something that is very important for many Muslim families. The Koran is kept on the highest piece of furniture in the room, and nothing is ever placed on top of it. It should never be allowed to touch the floor, and it is kept carefully wrapped when it is not being read.

Food

Like many other religions, Islam teaches that some foods are allowed, some are forbidden. Food which is allowed for Muslims is halal, food which is forbidden is **haram**. Anything that comes from an animal that eats other animals is haram, so is anything that comes from a pig. Fish and all fruit, grain, and vegetables are halal. To be halal, an animal that is to be eaten must be killed in a special way, so all the blood is removed. Allah's name is repeated to show that the food is being taken with his permission. The animal's throat is cut quickly with a very sharp knife, so that it becomes

Muslim children learn about their religion at home.

Muslims should only eat halal food.

tries, where many people's social lives involve going places that serve alcohol. Muslims believe that it is wrong to harm anything that Allah created.

THE IMPORTANCE OF TELLING THE TRUTH

There is a story that one day a man came to Muhammad and said, "O prophet of Allah, I have many bad habits. Which should I give up first?" Muhammad said, "Give up telling lies; always speak the truth." The man promised to do so.

That night, the man had planned to go out to steal. He thought of his promise, and knew that if he stole something, he would have to tell the truth to Muhammad about what he had done. So he gave up stealing. The next night, he planned to drink some wine. Muslims are not allowed to drink alcohol, and he knew that again he would have to tell Muhammad. So he gave up drinking alcohol.

One by one all his bad habits disappeared, because he had promised always to speak the truth.

unconscious from loss of blood. Muslims believe that this is the kindest way of killing there is. They feel it is much kinder than the usual Western methods of stunning by electric shock or a bolt fired into the skull.

If an animal is not killed correctly, anything from it is haram. This includes its fat, and because animal fat can be used in a whole range of products, these may also be forbidden. This can include things such as pastry, cake, and some cheeses. Food cooked in the fat of a haram animal becomes haram. Muslims who cannot buy halal products should eat only vegetarian products, because all these are allowed.

Alcohol is haram. That is why it is forbidden in Muslim countries. It is not really enough just to avoid drinking it themselves—Muslims should not be anywhere near when alcohol is being drunk. This can be a problem in Western coun-

MUSLIMS IN THE UNITED STATES

This section tells you something about Muslims in the United States.

The first Muslims to come to the West were Africans who came as slaves three hundred years ago. They could not practice their faith openly.

For a long time the Muslim population grew slowly. However, since the 1950s, the Muslim population has grown considerably. This is especially the result of immigration from Muslim nations of Africa and Asia. There are over three million Muslims in the United States today. Large mosques are found in many big cities, and many smaller cities now have mosques.

A Muslim family.

Many Muslims living in the U.S. were born here and have never lived in the country from which their families came. Many African-Americans have chosen to **convert** to Islam. Especially in the 1960s, the Nation of Islam, or black Muslims, grew in number. For some Muslims, life in the U.S. can be difficult. Their religion does not allow them to do some things which most Americans do, and Western standards—for example, in dress and behavior—are very different from the standards which are expected in Muslim countries.

Religion

Islam teaches that Muslims should obey the teachings of Allah in every part of life. This means that religion has much more effect on their lives than it has on many people brought up in the West. For example, Muslims pray five times a day. Muslims who work outside the home or who are traveling need a clean place in which they can pray, and time to be allowed for this. Sometimes this is misunderstood by employers who are ignorant of the religion. In public places it may mean being stared at or even laughed at by people who do not understand.

Dress

Islam expects both men and women to be decently dressed. For men this means being covered from the waist to the knees, for women it means that only hands and face should be visible to men who are not relatives. From about the age of 12, girls are expected to keep their arms, legs, and head covered. Sometimes this can cause problems at school, especially in gym and swimming.

Relationships

Muslim children are not expected to mix with the opposite sex once they become teenagers.

Young Muslim girls keep their legs covered for gym class.

This, too, can be a problem in school. Girls are not expected to go out alone with boys. When they wish to marry, their parents will help them to choose a partner because they care about them and have had more experience of life. Many young Muslims prefer to leave such an important decision to older relatives. They feel that the idea of going out with someone before marriage is like being in a market where people pick and choose the best product. Some young Muslims do not feel like this, however. They see friends choosing partners and feel that they should be able to do the same. This can cause enormous heartache for them and their families.

Medical treatment

Muslims do not think that it is right for a woman to be examined by a male doctor or a man by a woman doctor. If this is not understood, it can cause problems in the hospital, where there is usually no choice about which doctor sees a patient.

NEW WORD

Convert To become a member of a religion.

COMMENTS FROM A MUSLIM WOMAN LIVING IN ENGLAND

Being an English Muslim is not very easy. Although our numbers are growing daily, most of the Muslims in the UK are from other countries, and can support each other with their own ways, cultures, and languages.

Most people think it is very strange for an English person to become a Muslim, but really it is no more strange than being a Christian or a Jew. After all, Jesus, Muhammad, and Moses all came from the same part of the world. The hardest things are to change our diets, so that we only eat halal food; to give up alcohol and all social life that depends on alcohol; and to wear modest clothing. Most English Muslim women cover their legs by wearing long skirts or trousers, and wear long-sleeved blouses and a head scarf.

We pray five times a day, and do our best to show our faith in Allah by humble and helpful loving lives.

Author interview

SPECIAL OCCASIONS 1

This section tells you about the special things that happen to Muslim children.

Birth

Muslims believe that life is a gift from Allah. As soon as a baby is born, he or she is washed, and the adhan, the Call to Prayer, is whispered into the right ear. Then the Command to Worship is whispered into the left ear. This means that the first words a baby hears are the most important words of the Muslim faith. Then a tiny piece of sugar or honey is placed on the baby's tongue. This is a custom that comes from the Hadith and may be done by the parents or the child's oldest relative. Some people think it is a symbol of making the child "sweet," or kind and obedient.

Aqiqah

The **aqiqah** ceremony takes place when the baby is seven days old. According to the Hadith, a goat or a sheep should be sacrificed to give thanks to Allah for the arrival of the baby. At least a third of the meat is given to the poor. Today, animals may not always be sacrificed. Instead, a donation of money is given to the poor.

The baby is given its name at the ceremony. Choosing a name for the baby is one of the important duties of parents. Sometimes the name chosen is a family name, sometimes it is one of Muhammad's names, or one of his family. All Muslim names have a meaning. A common choice for boys is one of the 99 names of Allah, with "Abd" in front of it. Abd means servant in Arabic, so this is a way of saying that the child will be a servant of Allah. It is quite common for parents to stop using their own names when their first child is born and become known as "father of" and "mother of." For example, if the child was called Muhammad, the father would be known as "Abu Muhammad" and the mother as "Umm Muhammad."

At the aqiqah, the baby's head is shaved, and olive oil is sometimes rubbed in as a symbol of cleanliness. The hair which has been cut off is weighed, and the value of an equal weight in silver is given to the poor. Male babies are **circumcised** soon after birth. This means that the foreskin is removed from the end of the penis. It is quite a common operation.

Whispering the adhan to a new baby.

At the madrasah.

Attending the madrasah

From about the age of four, a child is expected to go to the **madrasah** regularly. This is the special school held at the mosque, where children learn to read and write Arabic, and recite the Koran. They are also taught the correct way to pray, and how to perform wudu, the special washing before prayers.

NEW WORDS

Aqiqah The naming ceremony.
Circumcision Removal of the foreskin from the penis.
Madrasah School at the mosque.

SOME OF THE 99 NAMES OF ALLAH

The Koran says that the most beautiful names belong to Allah.

The merciful;
the compassionate;
the forgiver;
the generous;
the affectionate;
the kind;
the gracious;
the protector;

the eternal;
the creator;
the holy one;
the mighty;
the wise one;
source of peace;
guardian of faith;
preserver of safety.

SPECIAL OCCASIONS II

This section tells you about special events which happen in a Muslim's life.

Marriage

Muslims are encouraged to marry, and few stay single all their life. Sexual relationships outside of marriage are disapproved of very strongly. Muslim marriages are usually arranged. (See page 38.) Both partners have to agree before the marriage can take place. The marriage ceremony is not a religious one. All the details of the marriage are set out in a contract, which is a legal document. It can contain almost anything that the couple wish to make a condition of the

An Indian Muslim bride and bridegroom.

marriage. (It could not include anything that would go against the purpose of marriage—for example, a condition not to live together.) The groom gives the bride a gift of money that remains hers even if he later divorces her.

The Koran says that a man can have up to four wives, but only if he can treat them all exactly the same. Today, this is usually seen as meaning that a man should only marry once, because it is obviously impossible to treat different people in exactly the same way. Some men do take a second wife, if the first cannot have children or becomes ill and needs someone to look after her. This can only happen if the first wife agrees. (It cannot happen in the United States, where marrying more than one person at a time is against the law.)

Divorce

Divorce is strongly discouraged in Islam, and it is often seen as a disgrace to the families if a marriage breaks down. Friends and relatives try hard to help a couple who are having difficulties. If divorce cannot be avoided, Muslim law says that the wife has the right to take all her belongings from the house. Once the divorce is final, her former husband has no further responsibility for her. She is usually looked after by her relatives because Muslim women are not encouraged to work. Muslims who have been divorced may marry again if they wish.

Death

If he or she can speak, the last words a dying Muslim will say are the Shahadah—"There is only one God and Muhammad is his prophet." After death, the body is washed and wrapped in white sheets, often the ihram sheets from Hajj. Muslims are always buried, never **cremated**. They believe that the body will be re-created and resurrected at the Day of

A Muslim funeral in Spain.

Judgment. Funerals should be simple, and Muslims prefer that the body should be in contact with the earth, rather than in a coffin. After prayers, the body is buried with the head and right side facing Mecca. If possible, Muslims prefer to bury a body on the day of death.

After death

Muslims believe in **akhirah**—everlasting life after death. They believe that this life is a test, and angels will tell Allah about the way each person has behaved on earth. Allah will then judge what each person has deserved. Those who have earned it will go to Paradise, a beautiful garden of peace, joy, and content-ment. Those who disobeyed and rejected Allah in their life on earth will go to **Hell** where they will suffer forever.

THE REWARD FOR FAITH

This passage from the Koran is part of a surah that describes what will happen after the Day of Judgment.

> *Those who have faith*
>
> *And do righteous deeds —*
>
> *They are the best*
>
> *Of creatures.*
>
> *Their reward is with Allah:*
>
> *Gardens of eternity*
>
> *Beneath which rivers flow;*
>
> *They will dwell therein*
>
> *Forever: Allah well pleased*
>
> *With them, and they with him.*
>
> *All this for such as*
>
> *Fear their lord and cherisher.*

Surah 98 : 7–8

INDEX

The numbers in **bold** tell
where the main definitions
of the words are.